I SELL TOMATOES

Inspiration and Consideration
Before End-Of-Life

Michelle Angel

trimarkpress

For my children
Uriah, Leyla, Jesse, Jessica

and grandchildren
Doruk, Kate, Collin, Quinn

You make my world a better place.

All stories that follow are true and based on personal experience of the author. Some names were changed or omitted to protect privacy, keep confidentiality, or for anonymity in order to honor and respect the deceased and all else involved.

Contents

Perfect Plan

You come with a birth date and a death date.
Everything in between is your destiny.
Your self-effort can change your destiny.

In other words,
You were born
when you were meant to be born,
you will die
when you are meant to die.
How you get from birth to death is up to you.
And it is all a Perfect Plan.

1
Introduction

I sell tomatoes. We'll get back to that. It's a better death and less fear I'm selling right now. Bear with me. Death really is my life.

Today you or someone you know might receive a life-threatening or terminal diagnosis. Or worse. Drop dead suddenly, without a hint of what hit. One way or another we can agree the end will come. No matter what the demise, wouldn't it be better to meet it fearlessly? Death is waiting all the time and so few of us are prepared. Not even a little.

I love death. That has to sound horrible to those that don't understand, but through the years I've gotten to know her. In spite of the bad rap, death is merciful and kind. Now dying, that's something else. This can be cruel and hard to endure, with as many facets as people. Dying is where I find my calling. It's still on this side of life. It's grounding in the depth of truth and the realness it demands. People are always inclined to ask me about *After*. Everyone wants to know what happens after, but for that I can only take you as far as the light – the rest you have to figure out for yourself. Know this though, *there is light* and *there is After*.

If each one of us has something special we are called to do in this life, as the wise have led us to believe, my unique talent is in being able to transition the dying. With death on my shoulder whispering in my ear, I'm guided to help those at end of life let go of the world they will leave behind, to face fearlessly what's ahead, the *After*.

Through the years, pastors and rabbis and hospice CEOs have all questioned how I do what I do. I can tell you for the most part, "I don't know." A part of me is left with my prayers and my shoes at the door of those I'm led to serve. Something beyond me happens when I'm called to a bedside.

THE FARMERS MARKET

Across the street from a city cemetery, a three-car garage was transformed into an oasis. Here people showed up, allured and enticed by the vibration of a place built with love and respect, offering the freshest and best of fruits, veggies, juices, flowers, baked goods and more. Here, at our Farmers Market, my adult son and I have welcomed and served the public for over twenty years.

For me the Market was the best of all worlds. It pulsed, vibrant with life, offering a balance to my time devoted to death.

Each morning at sunrise, before starting my day, I prayed silently: "If you want me to serve, show me how." With hundreds of people passing through our doors daily, the opportunity for me to talk death happened often. It was uncanny how frequently grief, death, and dying came up, which made me think, people do want to talk about it. As word got out that I did death work I often had those that sought me out in my little paradise jump through hoops so I could read their level of need and sincerity. Often purposely, I responded to inquiries with, "Where did you hear that? Death? I sell tomatoes."

BACK TO DEATH

This is not a book about Grief or After. (Although some of that is included). This is a book for before that. It is meant to encourage self-inquiry into the experience we're all guaranteed one day.

It was hard to pick and choose what to share in this little book. The subject matter is endless, but for practical purposes I have limited these pages to include Stuff Worth Mentioning (Chapter III) that might not otherwise be mainstream and ways to start the conversation about death and dying in order to develop a foundation for what's to come. Most importantly, and the reason for my work, I've included three very different experiences of light at death that affirm to me there is an After.

Death is not going away. We live in a time

in which everything gets researched to death, often excluding death. The fear of anything loses some of its power the minute it is made less confrontational. Perhaps that was the magic at the Farmers Market. There, surrounded by the breathing of life to its fullest, (ironically across the street from a cemetery), was a place where even conversations of death and dying felt non-confrontational, safe, and uplifting.

In the end (pun intended), the best deaths are the ones met fearlessly. I know this to be true. I invite the reader to be prepared and find out for themselves. If I can't sell that, there's always tomatoes.

Michelle Angel
Boynton Beach 2022

II
Light Story One

*If there was one common theme
that connected these
three stories of light,
it was gratitude and love.*

Bullshit - No Bullshit

When my brother Scott revealed he was diagnosed with AIDS,[1] the family was blindsided. It was 1989. Scott had just been married the year before and seemed to have a budding future in real estate. (Neither marriage nor career survived what was to follow.) My father took it the hardest. He couldn't stop crying, feeling overwhelmingly helpless at the

---

1. In the early 1980s the controversy surrounding the AIDS epidemic created fear as families were torn, physicians were stumped and the politics was full on impacted by finances and phobias. At this time, diagnosis of AIDS was a sure bet on death.

inability to overturn my brother's death sentence. Hopeless sadness embraced him with a magnitude of grief he was unable to shake.

Within a year's time, aggressive Cancer found its home in his once healthy lungs. It was heartbreak that helped it to spread quickly throughout his worn-down body.

My dad was diagnosed on a Tuesday. He died the following Monday.

BULLSHIT

Throughout my life, my father and I had a running dialogue that would usually end with an abrupt declaration of "Bullshit!" An expletive he used often. This end-of-life conversation was no different.

Now in a hospital hooked up to technology that was failing him, and being told, "Get business in order and gather family for final goodbyes," was more than a hint at the imminence. Breathless, he was barely able to get out a response in a whisper to his diagnosis. Through pursed lips, true to form, he managed a defiant, "Bullshit!"

Dangling was a medical possibility of buying time. (Later we found out doctors were getting paid per trial.) We heard, "Maybe two to three weeks, perhaps longer with treatment." Dad gambled on the "perhaps longer with treatment" and chose the poison. In retrospect, if we knew that two to three weeks would have been a gift, the choice might have been different.

Hours after the hopeful chemo was administered on his extremely compromised body, he suffered a massive stroke. Now, not only cancer stricken, he was also paralyzed and unable to speak. Dying took an ugly turn as death was upon us.

Morphine was begun and there was no turning back. Steeped in my belief that death as a finality doesn't exist, I continued with a dialogue meant for dying. Granted, at the moment, one sided.

"Daddy don't be afraid, you're safe Dad. Daddy you'll see a light, go to the brightest light Daddy... to the very brightest light you see." To this, with every ounce of life force he could muster up, like a deflating balloon with its last gasp of air, and before the morphine could settle in, he pushed out what would be his final word: "Bullllllllshit!"

Closing his eyes and turning away, he began his end. Saddened, loved ones retreated. I stayed, waiting for death's arrival.

In spite of the morphine coma he entered and with belief he could still hear me, I continued our dialogue. Silently and out loud. "You're safe Dad. I'm here Dad. You're not alone. You'll see a light Dad. Go to the brightest light, you'll see a light Dad..." I repeated the same words over and over. His response came without missing a beat. He couldn't speak but I could mentally hear my father loud and clear, in defense: "Bullshit! Bullshit! Bullshit!"

I watched the pattern of his breath change and his color fade. I moistened his lips, wiped his brow and aspirated the fluids that were pooling in the back of his throat. Two grueling days passed like this.

No Bullshit

Dad's breathing took a turn. I knew without knowing it was time. I called my aunt and mom from down the hall. They stood on one side of the bed while I faced them on the other.

With the quickness of a flash, and in a burst, the light in the room changed. Everything that followed seemed to happen at a snail's pace. It made sense to look towards the windows for the source, but the blinds were closed tight and the drapes drawn. Brighter. Way brighter. So much brighter than any light ever witnessed.

Light began to travel from the foot of the bed, up the white sheets pulled taut around my father's body. His muscular olive arms that rested outside the covers easily could deceive the unaware that this person was healthy. The light embraced over-folded, once strong hands, as it moved up his torso. We watched him raise his arm, outstretched now, elbow straight, reaching. Slowly, all so very slowly. Shoulders and neck were included, engulfed. The light lifted my father's head from under his chin, his face aglow as the brightness moved upward. Eyelids were open now. He appeared wide awake after a two-day, coma-induced deep sleep. His eyes were beaming in reflected brightness, as if seeing for the first time. In very slow motion my father turned to face me. Very, very slowly. Appearing deliberate.

Slowly he turned ... lowering his arm...

Smiling broadly now, his eyes locked mine.

Nothing else existed. All time stopped. I could see what he was seeing. Light radiated, reflected from him and around him. I could feel his thoughts. Gratitude was pouring out. Gratitude and love and light. For me. For all! I could hear everything he was thinking. And although we weren't speaking, intuitively we conversed. I spoke out loud and spoke without saying a word, and he heard me either way.

This light was like no other light. Not in color, not in strength, not in brightness, not like anything of this world light. Not blinding like the sun and yet brighter than. He silently questioned whether I could "see" what he was seeing. Our lifetime dialogue continued. "Yes, I see it." I said out loud to his internal inquiry. "The light Daddy. Yes Daddy, I see it too. Daddy I love you. Yes Daddy, the light." At the

same time, I laughed and cried gently. Joyous-
ly. "Thank you, Daddy. I see the light Daddy. Yes! Yes, I know Daddy...no bullshit," I
smiled. Thank you Daddy." I could feel immense gratitude and love from him, for him,
with him. He was affirming what I told him
to be the truth. The light. A gift. I thanked
him again.

As we witnessed together, in wonder and
awe, smiling, big broad, beaming smiles from
within, tears of ecstasy softly fell from us both.
Our silent dialogue continued as we witnessed
the light of eternity beckoning. Time was
non-existent.

And before I could realize this was *it* –
time for Goodbye Daddy, *it*, the ticking clock
and the measurement of minutes started up
again. The light lifted his head a bit more. He

looked away, and slowly facing forward, his eyes widened. He gazed into the beyond and that which awaited him.

Now no longer a part of my father's realm, I became aware of the presence of my mother and my aunt in the room.

Together we three watched the rise of his chest ever so slightly, breathing in his final link-to life. With no clinging, no fear, we witnessed the exhaling of his final breath, out.

With a poof – a gentle, peaceful poof – the light disappeared from the room, from my dad, from a lifetime.

His eyes still wide open, void of life, empty. We saw the light. No Bullshit.

Jack Angel 1928–1993

III

Stuff Worth Mentioning

*For the interested, there is a lot of
information on death, dying, and
grief. What follows is helpful stuff,
in brief, you may not have
come upon.*

AN AWAKENING

The suffering one experiences in dying, death and grief are catalysts to awaken to the truth of who you are. Go for the pain. On the other side is the joy your heart yearns for.

A GLIMPSE OF ETERNITY WITHIN

While studying the vastness of the universe a teacher helped me begin to grasp the concept of infinite by suggesting applying intellect to the depth of what one felt. Different from animals that feel and think, human beings' brains, a bit more evolved, can apply

one to the other. Yes of course! Fido might feel
and might even think. But Fido, with a frontal
lobe less developed than that of a human being,
cannot apply his thought to what he's feeling.

Infinite cannot be grasped by the mind
alone which measures in finite terms. Infinite
can be understood by applying the contempla-
tion of a feeling which has no boundaries. By
going to the depth of a feeling with thought,
the experience of infinite or eternity becomes
available within us.

LIVING WHILE DYING:
DENIAL, ACCEPTANCE, SURRENDER

Oddly, in death and dying, human nature includes denial as a way of acceptance. If

I deny death, I will be affirming life. Accepting death, I will die sooner.

To the contrary. Conceding that death is real, is more likely to affirm life.

As dying begins, holding death at bay, pretending the elephant in the room doesn't exist, walking on those proverbial eggshells, takes more energy and occupies more mental and emotional space internally than living in acceptance. That includes everyone involved. Honesty and truth have a way of breathing oxygen into where it's needed.

Discarding denial is a first step to power restored to those that feel powerless. The monumental energy that fear takes, once dumped, is used to fuel the life force. Extra fuel is what is needed to carry the human body a little further than perhaps it's capable of otherwise. Discarding denial buys time.

I've seen it a number of times. Living is extended beyond all predictions when acceptance is acknowledged. It's a shift of dying while dying to **living while dying**. There is a difference. Dying while dying usually has an eye on the future – death. Whereas living while dying remains present in real time. Live while you're dying and you won't miss a moment of life. *There's plenty of time to be dead!*

Surrender isn't giving up in this case. Surrender comes after acceptance and is when one begins to let go towards the bigger picture. Acceptance and surrender have no room for denial. Both are necessary for a conscious, liberating death.

It takes courage to speak the truth about death and dying. Done with love and compassion for one another, it uplifts and supports givers and receivers. Whether it be the dying person, the loved ones, or a professional involved, the fear of the unknown confronted, accepted and no longer denied, gives space, allowing for needed dialogue to meet an undeniable end.

Best to take a deep breath and say what's on one's mind. What's to lose? Dying comes with a real deadline.

THE MOMENT OF DEATH

The moment of birth and death are exactly the same moment. Both are ends and beginnings. The first breath in life is an inhalation.

The last sustaining breath is an exhalation.

In the moment between inhalation and exhalation, there is no past or future. Only eternity exists. After final exhalation that moment is presented as an opportunity. It is a portal for liberation.

CARETAKER FROM A DISTANCE

If someone you love is dying and you can't be with them physically it's a good time to connect with them energetically. The connect of a loved one goes way beyond the physical body.

Go someplace quiet. Disconnect from your head and let your heart take over. Being in nature is always powerful, but this exercise can be done from wherever you're standing.

Close your eyes. Take a few deep breaths. Hold the image of your loved one in your mind's eye. (The space between your eyebrows). Imagine yourself embracing this person (or pet).

Out loud or silently tell them they are safe, you are with them, you love them. Don't limit your words. Although nothing needs to be said. This is all about the love. Mentally hug - throw your arms around them. See yourself holding your loved one and they you. Do this for as long as you can, breathing in the essence that your memory holds of them. Feel it.

Shift to mentally putting a white light around them while letting them go from your mental embrace. Do this often. It's a protective white light of love. Don't forget to breathe. It's helpful if you practice this activity when the frustration or pain of separation shows up. It is far better to entertain thoughts of love and light instead of sadness or fear. In this way you are serving – doing the highest work for your loved one with whom there is physical distance and an energetic closeness. At end of life when the body is letting go this is perhaps what is needed most. Whether it be across the world or across the room.

The effort practiced here will also be quite effective in helping to feel connected after death.

HELP THE SOUL EXIT

It is believed the soul can stay in the body for up to four days after the vital signs are no longer detected. No worries. Eventually the soul figures out it's been evicted. After the moment of death the first place you should touch on the deceased is the top of the head. If the soul hasn't left, the energy of the touch will guide it to leave from the highest point of the body.

MISSING THE MOMENT

A huge percentage of people pass when their loved ones leave the room, even when loved ones have been intensely vigilant 24/7. Passing could occur when one leaves for a few minutes for a cup of coffee, for a bathroom break or a breath of fresh air. In a heartbeat – gone!

I've heard assumptions that "the dying

want to spare their loved ones of witnessing a frightening last breath," or that "the dying want to be left alone." Reality though, is that witness of the last breath is serene and gives closure. We confuse this idea of a frightening last breath when we don't witness it and are left to the fears that exist in our imagination. Additionally, when time is up, so are preferences. At the point of actively dying, the brain no longer functions the way it did before. Thought as we know it, is not the same. A desire to be left alone is not probable.

If the moment of death is missed after vigilantly sitting by a bedside for what feels like a lifetime, it is more likely that the energy between you became weaker and weaker as your loved one's body was breaking down. Like two magnets being pulled apart or getting distance between them, their pull no longer holds. Eventually the pull of death is stronger than that of life. By leaving the room you might be helping a loved one to let go. After death, sit with your loved one and say good-bye, silently or out loud.

49 DAYS

There are faiths that speak of a period after death (usually around 40-49 days) that the soul takes to settle into the next world. Certain cultures believe there is a shift in consciousness and even rebirth at this time.

It is in this period of time after someone dies that their soul is believed to stay close to this realm before moving on. During the first 49 days after death, it gives opportunity to do work for the departed. Every time you feel or think of the person who passed, address the deceased by their name. Tell them, "Go to the light. Go to the brightest light." Let them know you are OK. "The family is fine." Speak the names of family and friends. Using the name of the deceased is helpful as well. Say "Thank you" to the deceased as you tell them to "go to the brightest light, be free..." Send them off, let them go. This is especially helpful for suicides, violent deaths, sudden deaths, and any deaths that might have unfinished business, strong attachments, or confusion giving reason for the dead not to want to move on. Sometimes it's necessary to let the deceased know they are dead. It's always good to let them know their loved ones are OK. Addressing them this way can be helpful. No matter what the situation, expected or unexpected death, this period of time while doing work of an ethereal nature, is both healing for the deceased and the grieving. Although time is up for the body, this is work for the soul. Mark the time on a calendar from the day that the last breath was taken and feel the shift occur on day 49.

SIGNS

We have that moment when we think a loved one is contacting us from another realm. Butterflies or blue jays show up exactly when a connection is needed. It is a timely manifestation of what might otherwise seem impossible. The impeccable synchronicity of a moment or a meeting. Incidents of which are called signs.

When signs appear, give pause to the deceased that is linked to that sign. And then go beyond. Signs that appear to us are in answer to our needs and have a direct correlation with all universal energy. So, the interpretation of the butterfly you see isn't necessarily your loved one manifesting in a familiar physical form because they loved butterflies. It's bigger than that. It's the response of the entire universe. Yes, it's a sign, a reminder, an affirmation that your loved one's energy, melded with all other energy, including yours, is speaking to you in a way to make you pay attention. Embrace it. Take solace in it as a message and reminder from the universe. Everything is as it should be.

WHAT TO EXPECT

Near-death experiences offer similarities that would be hard to ignore. A tunnel and a bright light. Conversations and visits with the dead. Wind, ocean, flute, thunder, waterfall and humming – these all have been recalled as sounds heard leaving the body.

The wind in particular is an easy sound to become familiar with. No matter where you are – by the ocean, in a forest, on a cliff or at your back door – with eyes closed, listening to the sound of the wind can transport you in thought to other places where you've heard the same. As you become familiar with "the light" by observing and experiencing the sunrise (Chapter VII), you can also become familiar with the wind, a sound reported to be heard at death. This helps in the transition out of the body, making death a little more familiar and a little less scary.

GRIEF IS EXHAUSTING.
BE KIND TO YOURSELF.
GRIEF IS CUMULATIVE.

Grief takes place throughout a lifetime with every death and in some cases, loss not resulting in death, for example, a divorce or the loss of a job. Even life's passages, filled with transition and often a letting go of life as we knew it can cause a feeling of loss: graduating high school, starting a new career, having children, etc. Unprocessed, these feelings are compounded and what can appear as the grief for one event, might be the culmination of many experiences of loss. The source of feeling severely devastated by a particular death can be the result of loss that took place long before.

RE-DEFINING WHO WE ARE IN GRIEF

In grief you not only cry for the one that is gone, you cry for the loss of your own self. It is the part of you that was defined by the deceased. It is the piece of yourself that is identified through a glance. It is the intimacy we share with other human beings that tell us who we are. The more intimate, the deeper the loss. Your local grocer might be missed, but the level of intimacy is nowhere near the level of intimacy and loss one feels of an immediate family member.

You walk into a room and your mom,

whether a good or bad parent, is someone with whom you share the intimacy of history. With just a glance, she defines "the you" without any effort on your part. No one else on the planet will define you the same. When she's gone, that piece of yourself, that connects to yourself on the deepest level, also feels gone.

This phenomena isn't just left to the loss of people. All relationships, good and bad, define us beyond the obvious – work and homes, places, things and stuff. And with pets, the loss of unconditional love that goes very deep can be devastating.

The good news is you never felt anything that wasn't within. It's a matter of reconnecting with your own self.

GRIEF AND THE PHYSICAL WORLD

To bereave literally means to be deprived by death. So yes, they're in a better place and free. Yet no matter how much faith and certainty in that, the reality remains that we live in a physical world determined a great deal by our senses. We want to see them, hear them, smell them, taste them and touch them.

VISIT THE MEMORIES

The tendency in grief is to reflect on the period of dying before death. Know this will cause more pain. Try to go back to a more pleasant time in life.

Visit with your loved ones in your memory. I like to do this before bed, but anytime works. Contemplate to recall. Sometimes it takes a few tries to jog one's memory. The more details the better this exercise gets. It's not hard, and done right, the memory can be so vivid that opening your eyes again, back into the current reality can be painful. With practice the pain dissipates and the memory relived results in pure delight.

IV

Light Story Two

*In the early 1980s the controversy
surrounding the AIDS epidemic
created fear as families were torn,
physicians were stumped, and the
politics was full-on impacted by
finances and phobias. At this time,
diagnosis of AIDS was a sure
bet on death.*

The Soul's Exit

Seven months after my father's death, my grandfather died. In spite of his age of ninety-five, his death was preceded and caused, like my dad, by the loss of his son and a broken heart. My brother Scott's health began going downhill soon after. It was a slow tortuous decline that lasted for the next seven months. My sister and I began spending more time with him in Manhattan, until visiting wasn't enough, and I moved into his studio apartment in the clouds on the 18th floor. Together we prepared for what was to come.

AIDS is like a tornado in the body. As soon as one horrible assault from the attack on the system was addressed, another popped up. Adding to the urgency of putting out fires and guessing at the diagnosis were the side effects from drugs that were mostly experimental. My brother Scott suffered through vomiting, incontinence, atrophy and neuropathy, fevers, blistering, night sweats, coughing up blood, anxiety, emotional tears and lesions that caused agony and cries of pain from the first breath in the morning till the last at night. His AIDS-related dying was a nightmare. Death would be welcomed. We were reaching the end of a long, heart wrenching journey.

TRANSITION

At the end of daylight, the transition of breath changed quickly. Scott's labored breathing was racing, as his temperature spiked to 105. His inability to swallow meant finding an alternative to getting the pain drugs he needed into him.

Nurses were showing up from all over the world to serve where needed in the AIDS epidemic. Erin was from Ireland, sent today from hospice to check on us. And not a minute too soon. She was kind and caring. It took a bit to adjust to the brogue though. *"Waaat 'av yer girls dahne 'ere?"*

My sister and I gave each other questioning looks before she continued. *"It's so peacefoehl. So very peacefoehl. Beautifoehl. Yer girls ded good."* Her sing-songy voice was soothing. She was soothing. Gently caring for Scott, respectfully with love, she made us all comfortable. Arming us with instruction, suppositories of Morphine and Tylenol and the possibility that this stage of *"dyin cooehld go fahr a few days,"* she left. An angel of mercy, off to minister to another. My sister left after Erin, to catch the last train out to Long Island.

And there we were. Scott and I. Late now. After 10 p.m. Scott panting. A sound and a pace that although assured normal, was somewhat alarming. I laid out my sleeping bag on the floor next to his bed, setting an alarm to give him aspirin two hours after the 11 p.m. dose of Morphine. I wasn't willing to risk a high fever that could lead to seizures if I missed a dose. I kissed him gently goodnight. His brow was moist and lips were dry. Watching the labor that came before death, praying, meditating, I hadn't meant to sleep.

The contrast of the sound of his panting and fighting for air to the quiet and stillness woke me with a start. I don't recall getting to my feet, but there I was standing by his side. Candles flickered. The digital clock read 12:08 a.m. I had missed my brother's last breath.

Taking a moment to adjust to the light, I took in the scene we had planned for. His mouth slightly hanging open, formed, as if to say ahhhhh. A nose that no longer flared while gasping. His eyes half open, half-closed slits. The lack of movement in his chest. The complete quiet of a life ceased. Taking it all in, I felt the calm. I was ready. I remembered to touch the top of his head first, knowing that if his soul was stuck, it would be guided by the energy of my hand and leave from the highest point of his body. Now I was checking vitals. His limbs were still warm. I made the necessary calls to family and hospice. The body would be taken care of the next day.

I sat on my makeshift bed on the floor and faced my brother's still body. As I adjusted to the silence that replaced the struggle for breath, the awareness now of his presence hit. He had stopped breathing, all his vitals had gone cold, and yet I could feel his familiar essence. He was dead, but he was there with me. "Oh Scott, be free brother," I whispered.

Taking a meditation position, closing my eyes, inhaling deeply, exhaling the same, I effortlessly entered another state of being. Deep. Very deep. Time passed. I don't know how much time. Until it began.

I heard the guttural sound before feeling it. I attempted to clear my throat. And could not. The need became greater and greater as words came deep from within me, but were not of me. I addressed my brother. First quietly, whispering, "Spirit of Scott, spirit of Scott." Louder. A talking voice. "Spirit of Scott. Go to the light. Spirit of Scott go to the brightest light."

Repeated again. Louder. Out of my control, my voice got louder.

Deafening.

The voice was commanding. Louder.

"SPIRIT OF SCOTT. GO TO THE BRIGHTEST LIGHT. SPIRIT OF SCOTT.

GO... GO.

GOOO TO THE BRIGHTEST LIGHT.

"GO!"

Voice loud, very loud. "GO TO THE BRIGHTEST LIGHT. SPIRIT OF SCOTT!"

Yelling, chanting, frenzied.... "SPIRIT OF SCOTTT YOU ARE THE LIGHT!!! GO TO THE BRIGHTEST LIGHT! YOU ARE THE LIGHT! THE BRIGHTEST LIGHT! SPIRIT OF SCOTT!"

Repeated over and over.

"Spirit of Scott!" Chanting.

Then it stopped. It took a moment to regain my breath. There was loss of all time. My eyes were now wide open.

"Where did I go?" I thought, regaining myself. "How loud was I? Possessed? And by what?"

With a deep breath, in spite of all the prep, knowing that he was free, that death was better for Scott, I was sad, for just a moment, at the sight of my brother's dead body. Astonished, the dialogue with myself continued. "What?" asked my eyes as I whispered out loud. What was I seeing? Something moved in his chest. It was rising, the whole chest at once. Not like in a breath. It was more of a bulge, growing from inside him, creating a noticeable bump. It was pushing while moving upward, as if it were trying to find a way out. I watched as it traveled from between his ribs, finding its way towards his throat. Steadily. Slowly. I watched. Stunned, silently asking myself, "What the ...?" And then the bulge pushing against his throat headed towards his mouth. Something red was emerging. I could see just a little light. Then, it appeared to be flames escaping over my brother's lips. As I watched in confusion, a spinning fireball exited his gaping mouth. Like a pinwheel at high speed in the wind, it spun intensely. Speeding fast, yet standing still. Spinning so fast there was a tail of light in its wake. Fire spinning fast, fast spinning fire. And then slowing. Cooling. Its scarlet rim thinning. The flames disappeared and the fireball changed from red hot to celestial shades of blue. I was pulled in by the light, the beautiful, illuminating light shining from this, that left my brother. I watched as it traveled above Scott's still body, changing its color while moving and cooling. Stopping between the navel and the heart, about a foot above, there it hovered. Emitting its own light, it appeared vibrantly alive. I was mesmerized. White light now poured from this illuminated sphere connecting to my brother. There was an intense knowing and intimacy emanating from brilliant beams directed at the body. I felt immense gratitude and love showering the once inhabited home. I witnessed in awe, paused in a moment of eternity, clear now as to what I was seeing. The soul was thanking its body. It was a heartfelt farewell. Not lasting long, and without warning, in a dart, whooooosssh. It disappeared.

After waking my loved ones for a second time that evening, to share the experience of witnessing the soul's departure, I bid my brother goodnight before kissing him on his now cold cheek. As I fixed the blanket snugly around his stiffened body, the noticeable presence of death that permeated our home for many days was noticeably gone, as was Scott.

Lying on my bed on the floor, a deep, sweet sleep came before meeting the dawn of a new day and an embrace of the epiphany revealed. I felt called to serve the dying. This was my work.

Scott Angel 1959-1994

V

The Bigger Picture

"When a man dies, he does not just die of the disease he has: he dies of his whole life."

- *Charles Péguy 1873-1941*

Rarely do we get to see the bigger picture as it's taking place. In order to see, one must move out of the comfortable position of just viewing what's going on in our own, immediate, little world. Everything effects everything else. It's that pebble in the pond example. Something so little as a pebble, causing a wave of motion. When looking bigger it puts serendipity in its place as not a phenomenon that stands on its own, but with dependency on many other things. It is recognizing that random clearly has a purpose, however concealed, it is somehow still connected to what came before and what will follow.

Glimpses of the bigger picture give affirmation to the infinite plan of the universe, which ultimately shows the humbling importance we all hold. Everything matters- even when you feel like you're just going through the motions. What you do has meaning. One person's actions can make a difference. We all are connected, responsible for that ripple effect.

Here is the bigger picture: Everything you have done in your life has led to this moment. Look back an hour, a day, a week, a month, a year, ten years, a lifetime, perhaps many lifetimes, all leading to you reading these words at this very moment. Can you see how one moment has been necessary for the next?

Maybe you got here consciously in search of, or not. And just perhaps, you will open up to one passage that speaks to you and gives you just a tad more understanding about death and dying. Or maybe words that you come across will help a friend. Who knows? Maybe this is just a stop along the way connecting you to what's next. None-the-less here you are now. That is the bigger picture.

BACK BURNER

How we end up in each others lives, is a mystery solved by the bigger picture.

It was in 2005 that I offered my time to workshops about death and dying at Gilda's Club[2]. At one workshop I met Ryan who lost his partner to cancer. Years later, he contacted me when he lost his dog, through health issues, more loss, and a move to San Francisco. He's one of many I've met along the way that

---

2. Gilda's Club was founded in 1995 and named for Gilda Radner (1946-1989), an original cast member of *Saturday Night Live*. Gilda's Club Mission is dedicated to ensuring that all people impacted by cancer are empowered by knowledge, strengthened by action and sustained by community. All services are free.

keep me on the back burner, calling as needed when death or grief show themselves. Now ten years after Gilda's, he called about Mandy, an old work buddy who was very ill. She lived in Boston, but was visiting her old stomping grounds in Lauderdale for final good-byes. By the time she called it was almost time for her to return to Boston. (They want to see me, but they don't.)

It was slow and difficult for her to move as she led me up a stairwell away from the activity of the living. It gave me time to silently assess. I could feel the presence of death around her which gave me pause as to what was keeping her. With distended belly caused by a winning cancer she looked about six months pregnant, just a little bit of a thing. Her face was drawn, beautiful, with piercing aqua eyes that twinkled like bright stars popping against a dark sky.

Barely body, mostly soul coming through. It appeared Mandy was living beyond her destined time.

Emotionally stuck at end of life, she needed help sorting out how to live and move forward. I listened. We spoke of yesterdays, todays and tomorrows. Much inner work was done apparently. Death and dying wasn't her issue. She knew where she was going. Living was Mandy's issue. Life was not letting her go although she appeared ready. It was my job to find what was holding her. And quickly. She cried about losses. Babies and lovers. Mostly Richard. "My soul mate. A hole ripped through my heart when he died." They never married. She was a little sad and angry with some regret. A shift of perspective quickly transpired and she forgave her lover and herself. There was obvious work left to do. Richard's business needed closure. Richard's ashes that still sat by her bedside needed to be scattered. Stuff she owned, needed to be dealt with, given away and donated. I gave permission, that she really didn't need to let go of what wasn't doable. We spoke of her final memorial plans. I gave pointers on dying.

When Mandy was back in Boston we spoke a few times after our initial meeting. With each call I was surprised she was still alive, believing she was pushing her death date. She had completed what she set out to do. She was weak and she was tired, contented as well.

It was a few months after we had met that I received a call from someone identifying herself as Mandy's nurse. "Mandy is at end of life and can hardly speak, but wanted to hear your voice." She held the phone to her patient's ear. Mandy spoke in a whisper.

"I'm afraid."

"Nothing to be afraid of," I said. "You've done this before." (Referring to her belief in the cycle of life and death).

"OK."

I could feel the effort it took to blow out that little word. "They'll all be there to meet you. Your dad, the baby you lost, old friends and Richard. Richard will be there."

"Yes." she faintly responded.

"My darling, you are safe, stay calm." I continued, "The light will be very bright. When it appears you just have to move towards it. It's about the love. You'll be entering love. Feel the love Mandy. Can you feel it?" I continued without expecting a verbal response. "Close your eyes Mandy." I spoke very calmly, slowly. "Bring your breath from your toes... up through your legs... the trunk of your body. Feel the breath in your belly... in your chest. In your heart.

Move it upward to the crown of your head. Remain calm. Let it fill your head... release it from the top of your head, your mouth, your nose. Mandy, you just need to breathe. Remain calm. Deep breath in, from your toes. Draw it up. Deep breath out through your head. Again. Deep breath in. From your toes, bring the breath up to your head. Deep breath out. You're not alone Mandy. You can do this. Just breathe deep. You are the light Mandy."

From the other end of the phone I could hear an acknowledging. A surrendering acceptance that came in the sound of a "hmm."

"See you on the other side my friend. Have a great journey," I replied.

The nurse, taking the phone from her patient's ear, thanked me and hung up. Ten minutes later she called back. Mandy had passed.

Mandy 1955-2015

BOWL, BOTOX, BOY-FRIEND
& A MORAL OF THE STORY

At this time, the Market was thriving and my job was more social than anything else. My son had taken over almost all the logistics of the day-to-day business and my work was left mostly to two areas. The cut flowers and keeping an eye on the front of the house. I mingled with the customers, welcoming folks into my home away from home, making sure everyone got what they needed, and then some. I'd jump behind the register when an extra pair of hands was needed to move the lines more quickly.

The story that follows took place, over almost thirty years.

THE BOWL

In the eighties Michaela and I were both new mothers. She was a birth educator and I taught infant massage. Our bohemian-like lifestyle, coupled with our similar roots were part of a common recipe that connected us. One day she showed up at my door. Her Volkswagen van was packed to the brim and two children were neatly strapped in. She was leaving her alcoholic husband, her home in Coconut Grove, and heading west to California like a modern-day pioneer. We hugged as she handed me a beautiful wooden salad bowl. It came with instruction. "Please keep this for me. It's my mother's and she'd kill me if I left it behind."

We lost touch. Relationships were kept by mail or phone-land lines in those days. Twelve moves between us, in and out of about five states, and over twenty-five years later, at the Market now, I stepped out front for just a moment to help the cashier, when I saw her. And she me. And with no regard to the busyness around her at the moment, in her best Bronx, Michaela exclaimed loudly over the heads of the customers that separated us, "Do you have my mother's f-ing salad bowl?"

"Yeah." I laughed and added, not caring about the onlookers, "I've been schlepping that f-ing thing for twenty-five years!"

Our friendship continued where it left off as if no time between us had ever lapsed.

BOTOX

It was about a year later that Michaela was in town again from Santa Rosa. Her mother who lived down the street from the Market (and who's salad bowl I had kept for twenty-five years) was bedridden, with hospice on board. Michaela having to head back home, asked me to support her sister Stephanie in the difficult responsibility of her mother's end.

Stephanie and I became fast friends, bonding while navigating the emotions and logistics of letting go. Over the heartfelt conversations about everything from feeding tubes to freeing souls we shared in the intimacy of her mother's death.

*Life, even when tenuous, is still on
this side of living. There's still the warmth of a body
and the rhythm of the breath
that connects us.*

The passing now was imminent. Through the night, while my friend Michaela was mak-

ing her way back east in the sky, and her sister
Stephanie slept soundly on a twin bed in the
same room as her dying mother, their mom,
ever so quietly, slipped away.

*Even when dying is difficult
and long and death is expected and welcomed
the finality is always profound.*

The sun was just rising as we got ready for
another day at the Farmer's Market. I was fill-
ing buckets of water for flowers when Stephanie called. Able to drop everything, I was by her
side within minutes. Stephanie and I held hands
quietly taking it in.

*Saying goodbye takes on
a whole new meaning at death.*

Encouraging Stephanie to leave her mother's dead body, to take a shower and get ready for what promised to be a busy day ahead, I continued with silent prayers.

The aide that was in the living room during her mom's exit had joined us. Entering the room in a robe, drying her hair with a towel, Stephanie looked up exclaiming, "OH MY GAWD! It looks like my mother got BOTOX!" It took a moment to see it, the way Stephanie saw it, before we all burst out laughing. It was true. Her mother's face prior, pained and tense, now looking sublimely at peace. Beautiful.

The mortician would say pallor mortis had set in. The physical change in the body that comes soon after death when the muscles become relaxed and limp. Personally, I think it was an indication that the soul left the body.

Gloria 1930-2017

Boy-Friend

Another year passed when Michaela called from California in regard to an old boyfriend she had known since she was five. Steven was dying in a state-run nursing home conveniently located one town north from the Market. "'Would you look in on him?" she asked. "He has a big persona. The go-to guy and salt of the earth." She added sadly, "He's alone."

Steven was bedridden in a room pushed to the back of the facility where a few hospice beds drew Medicaid dollars. Unfortunately, hospice training wasn't included. His body was mangled, bloated, toothless. His skin sallow and pitted. Cancer wasting, with diabetic complications, doesn't exactly pretty anybody up. It only took a moment though to look past the exterior.

The first week we teased and tested through

playful banter while figuring out our common ground. I listened while he told his story. He generously wanted to know mine.

I found myself looking forward to our time together. His genuine happiness to see me when I arrived for a visit was reflected in a boy-like smile that lit up his face and seemed to tone down the drama surrounding us. I liked when he smiled. It made me feel loved, in a way that was unfamiliar and wonderful to receive.

The second week was a little more serious, less talk, and more focused on end of life. The decline was fast. Pain meds increased, making conversations now unfinished, as his thoughts would drift. Mortality was confronted while we laughed, cried and faced it together. This was a love affair that as fate would have it, would end at death do us part. Soon.

By week three, Steven became quieter. I was

only getting a slight smile for my playful greeting of, "You're still here!" Just a week prior, we'd laugh over his quick-witted responses.

Under the guise that I was Steven's family, giving me access to medical decisions, I began to take charge. I closed his door often, but we could still hear the cries of the unattended at all hours. As Steven's voice became weaker mine became stronger. He needed protection from unqualified aides who in their ignorance were abusive. I walked in on force feeding, when he was no longer able to swallow, and the avoidance of changing soiled bedclothes and linens causing a stench and the beginnings of bed sores. I fought, yelling at everybody and anybody for the long worn-off pain meds that weren't given on time due to apathy that comes from a hardening to suffering. There would be no unnecessary pain under my watch. Showing up unannounced, at all different times gave me more opportunity to see incompetence and failure of proper care in action. It wasn't personal, just bad business. Understaffed, poorly run facilities are terrible places for the dying without an advocate. They didn't like me at the nursing home. I knew that would be the case going in.

As the disease was winning it quieted us both. I spent our days lying next to him in his hospice bed. Old friends, so it appeared, head-to-head, we shared earphones and listened to rock and roll together while he drifted in and out. His time was nearing.

Barely breathing, eyes closed, he faintly whispered, "See you on the other side." Those would be his last words. Still needing protection, at the mercy of what appeared to be a God-forsaken place, I stayed. Lights bright, TV blaring in the room he shared, I was reminded of the lack of respect given at this intimate time. What I could control, I did.

No more being jabbed, being moved and jostled. No more. I was there to serve his laboring. I called his parents by their names, Leona and Max, and told him they were waiting. He lightly pressed his thumb into my hand in response.

I kept his forehead cool, body lightly covered, lips moist and mind calm. Assuring him throughout he wasn't alone. He was safe. I believe that reassurance is what the dying need most. Protecting his immediate space, I watched and listened while his chest grew more congested and his pace of breath changed. First deep, heavy and rapid, he labored this way for what felt like forever. Then his breathing finally slowed to little bird breaths. Small gulps of air. The sign he was going. Placing my hand on the top of his head he heaved, sighed, and with great effort, gave two more slight sighs. The last exhale was with every remaining bit of life. A barely noticeable breath and he was gone.

After sitting with him for as long as the staff would allow, I watched them prepare my friend's stiff body for removal, making ready the space for another.

All deaths are different for me. Most are uplifting and filled with the elation of a soul free. Reflecting on the chain of events that led me to be at Steven's death and the gratitude I felt at the moment, I had the additional thought of what if we had met at another time. Reminding myself, perhaps we had, or perhaps we will.

Steven 1951- 2018

THE MORAL OF THE STORY

Even the exchange of a simple salad bowl can have long-term meaning. Everything is connected. How do we end up where we end up when we end up? And why? To the last question – the bigger picture.

Long before a farmers market that was my happy home for twenty years. Long before I met Michaela or Ryan – the seeming connections for the dying I would serve. Long before a calling whispered in my ear, igniting a passion that had been there always. Long before and long after, through life and death, it is often hard to see, but always a given, always unfolding: the bigger picture.

VI
Light Story Three

It was years after I saw the light at
my father's death and the soul leave
my brother's body that Keb came
into my life. Giri and I spoke
over the counter, while I was bagging her
groceries at the Market. It wasn't
the first time we spoke, but it was
the first time she mentioned her
husband, at end of life, who might
be feeling afraid. She hoped perhaps
I could help. I was going overseas
the next day, but I promised to visit
when I returned. If it was meant,
Keb would still be alive, a sign I was
intended to serve him.

Into The Light

good sign:

A bigger-than-life-size Buddha was at the entrance of their home.

When I met Keb he was bedridden. Grossly thin, his face drawn, he appeared small in stature. Probably not the Keb his friends and family knew. The only Keb I would ever know. The physical body was now a transparent casing that couldn't hide the light that shone so brightly from within him. To me he looked transcendent.

I recognized him immediately. Perhaps someone I had traveled with in some other lifetime. We were old friends from first introduction. Our backgrounds and the paths we explored were similar in our search. We were almost the same age, and had grown up on Long Island, with similar cultural beginnings. Our deep connection to eastern philosophy, the belief in one fundamental truth, and finding our way to Yoga Ashrams, rich in Hinduism, was paralleled. I so appreciated the work he did. Bar Mitzvah, Buddha, Ashrams and yoga. The breath. He knew about breathing. Soul searching. Soul finding. He was ready and open for final instruction to have the best possible death. He believed in liberation from the cycles of birth and death. He didn't want his fear or unfinished emotional business to get in the way.

I prayed as I entered the relationship for the wisdom to give Keb what he needed. We began at first meeting. Not knowing it would be three weeks before his final breath, still there was no illusion about the lack of time. The work started with the remembering and reminding. "In the end the only thing that is real, the only thing that ever mattered is the love." In the end only the love. We repeated often. In the end only the love! It is what we take and what we leave behind. It put it all in perspective. They were grounding words needed as the physical was slipping away.

In the weeks that passed I talked as Keb listened. Keb talked as I listened. And in between the work we did together was Giri, selflessly, supportive in every way.

Keb, cornered because he was bed-bound, with a home-school teacher, me, would say with a smile, "You talk so much." And I gently reminded him, yielding to his pace, "There is much to learn, to get through, to let go of, to finish, to be ready for, so as to have the best death." Hard as it was, he never stopped me, as he wanted what I was selling and respected that tomorrow may not come.

Calmly, Keb would lie back and graciously nod through question and dialogue that was intended to go deep. Crossing his arms over his chest, with great conviction he would say, "I understand." Two little words became my sign that he got it and I could move on. Making me smile in his seriousness, he reminded me of Yul Brynner in *The King and I*.[3] Can you picture it? "I understand" is what every teacher strives

---

3. *The King and I*: A musical by Rodgers and Hammerstein (1951) based on the novel *Anna and the King of Siam* by M. Landon (1944)

for. He was determined, having faith in the real possibility of meeting the goal. Eternal freedom.

Three weeks passed since our first meeting. The level of intimacy granted to me by this unique couple was humbling. Keb kept things intense with his seriousness. Giri kept things light and balanced with her sense of humor and generosity of spirit.

Wednesday before his death, Keb mustered up all expendable energy for a final business transaction that had been pending for months long before his illness. It would be conducted over the phone from his death bed. Once completed, now totally life exhausted, he rested.

Thursday the quiet began to set in. There was little to talk about. He was ready. By the evening I found my own silence. As Keb half watched TV distracted by his own thoughts, me nearby, he questioned, "Why so pensive?"

"Nothing left to say." I smiled. Keb met me with his final Yul Brynner nod, and said, "I understand. It's all about the love." I kissed his cheek as I left.

"Sweet boy," I said. "They're waiting for you." He nodded, whispered, "Thank you, I love you." And me right back at him. "Thank you. Thank you. I love you too."

The next day Giri let me know that Keb's breathing had shifted. It was Friday. I was busy tending retail. It was season at the store, which meant snowbirds[4] were showing up from the north. Snowbirds were the first sign in the south that we were entering winter. Weekends were especially hectic. Business kicked up to double the clientele in just a few short weeks. It demanded longer hours, more product, and

---

4. Snowbirds is a name given to the people that come to Florida in the winter months.

more employees to manage the influx.

I got to Keb and Giri's late. He was resting peacefully with his wife at his side. Calm permeated. His breath was shallow and steady. Keb had begun the process of transitioning labor. I sat with him going over final instructions about what to look for, what to listen for, about his breathing, about the light... the many lights. Now his "I understand" became a slight nod of his head and a slow blink of his eyes. When it was time to leave and bid my friend farewell, his eyes reflected acknowledgment and readiness. He searched and practiced for a lifetime to meet this moment. It all felt very humbling.

The next morning, Saturday, perhaps Sabbath in some other life, completing what it took to open the Market, I was preparing to look in on Keb when Giri called to say he had passed.

I arrived very shortly after, stopping to

pranam[5] to the Buddha that welcomed the entrance of their home and the Hindu deities that lined the path to Keb's bedroom. On the way, I took energetic inventory, and knew what I was feeling. Bowing my head to Keb's still body I observed his skin an ashen blue, his jaw slightly hanging open, and the noticeable beauty he maintained in spite of vitals that had stopped. And there was more. Keb was still around. I could feel his presence. His soul hadn't left yet.

Without words, Giri and I acknowledged each other. She rose from the chair by her husband's head and sat by the foot of his bed. With a nod, I took the empty chair and a meditation position.

Closing my eyes, I easily found the depth of peaceful silence. Only to be disrupted by a sound that came from my throat. It was reminiscent, yet unfamiliar. Guttural and rough. Not too

5. Pranam: a respectful greeting or farewell made by touching one's palms together.

loud, nor too soft. Just above a whisper. I could feel the sounds. I could hear them. Repeating.

They were sounds I could feel in my gut but coming from my throat. I spoke, quietly at first, then louder, until a crescendo of words came through me, not from me. *Through* me.

"Spirit of Keb, spirit of Keb, SPIRIT OF KEB , don't look back, DON'T LOOK BACK! Spirit of KEB, don 't look back, DON'T LOOK BACK, don't look back. SPIRIT OF KEB don't look back!" Calling those words pleading, intensely... "SPIRIT OF KEB! DON'T LOOK BACK! SPIRIT OF KEB... " Maybe for a minute or two. I don't know. Time went unmeasured. It stopped. The space around me disappeared. "Spirit of Keb, Spirit of Keb..." and as the words filled me, filled the room, I found myself fervently in urgent repeating of this call. Until...

In my mind's eye I saw the light.

A GIANT RADIANT BALL OF LIGHT
WAS RISING.
So, Sooo BRIGHT!
Brilliant Bright. Blazing.
It rose from darkness like the sun
on a clear horizon.
Intensely white bright,
spreading it's light...

And there was Keb. Standing in front of this ball of light. He faced it full on. His back to me. His long curly gray locks flying behind him. He was dressed in what appeared to be the sparse loincloth of a Sadhu.[6] One foot was on the ground with his other foot placed high

---

6. Sadhu: a term for an ascetic or someone who practices yoga. The sadhu is solely dedicated to achieving liberation.

on his thigh with knee pointing straight out.[7]

I watched as his arms lifted from in front of him and reach to the sky. Reaching, fingers grasping at the divine. On two legs, then one. He was dancing in this way, in ecstasy. Back and forth swaying like a palm tree in a breeze. And all the time I chanted passionately, with intensity that wasn't my own. "Spirit of Keb, Spirit of Keb, Spirit of Keb don't look back, don't look back. Spirit of Keb don't look back. Don't look back, don't look back! Spirit of Keb. DON'T LOOK BACK!"

And as I chanted, cheering him on, I watched his joyful, rhythmic motion. His raised arms swayed gloriously. Standing before the light, reaching to the heavens! Watching his

---

7. Tree pose: Done by foot placed high on thigh with knee pointing straight out to the side. It is a balancing position that is still one of the very few standing poses from medieval Hatha Yoga and popular in modern times.

ecstasy, experiencing joy unencumbered, my tears began to flow. Smiling ear to ear I watched as Keb danced euphorically. Swaying, reaching.

As I bear witness, Keb danced, dissolved, disappeared, vanished right into that blazing luminous ball, with total abandonment to the world behind, and with total surrender to the world ahead. I watched as he was surrounded and swallowed up. Not a trace. In an instant Keb was gone. And like that, so was the light.

It took me a moment to be back in the room with Giri and Keb's vacant body. Opening my eyes, I turned to Giri. "I have to tell you what I just saw." She listened intently and took a deep breath before she shared. "Just before Keb died, he was making some sound I couldn't understand. Also guttural, throaty." She asked her husband over and over, "What is it Keb? What is it?"

She went on, "Raising his arms, he opened his eyes really wide, a giant smile on his face. He lowered his arms across his chest. And then he looked towards me," said his devoted wife, "he closed his eyes and soon after took his final breath."

Keb's energy once felt in the house was now lifted. Giri and I hugged, laughed, cried, and marveled at the similar experiences we had *before* and *after* death.

Keb was free. And although he was gone, his love, undeniably remained.

Keb 1952-2018

VII

Let's Talk

Many believe by talking about the inevitable they will somehow be abandoning hope and betray the dying, all while beckoning closer what they avoid. Old school superstition held belief that just the mention of the "D" word awakens Death itself.

I can remember as a small child my great grandmother having me spit off my tongue, as if poison, any talk of the "D" word. She believed even a whisper would draw one's demise closer, inviting bad luck and the Grim Reaper. Fortunately, talking about death is getting better. Not that long ago the "C" word was handled in the same way, whispered as if mention would cause the disease to just spring up. Now cancer, its treatments, and drugs are spoken about and advertised like breakfast cereals.

Contrary to old superstition, people do want to talk about it. They want to talk about death and dying and loss and grief. We all want answers as to what's the point? None of us want to be alone, or in pain at end of life. We all want to know where we'll be in the after.

With the level of intimacy that death conversation demands we often feel we're alone, but truth be known, everyone has a story and everyone wants to tell it.

Build Your Foundation

A good foundation is meant to hold a structure upright through forces of nature.

Build your personal foundation with the answers to the questions you shouldn't wait to ask. The big questions, about life and death and dying. These answers tell you who you are.

When life throws you something difficult or unexpected and your foundation is in place, you'll only have to address the issue at hand, without the confusion and added burden of figuring out where you stand in life. You won't be faced with the big questions while trying to weather a storm or while putting out a fire. When chaos or crisis ensues, it's not the time to be asking yourself what you believe in.

It is often too late to build your foundation when turbulent forces of nature are upon you.

Better to build when your world is calm and clear.

Practice "Perfect Plan"

These two little words, "Perfect Plan," give faith to a foundation. Practice "Perfect Plan" in good times, bad times, and all times while the bigger picture unfolds. In this way the mind will be trained to go to "Perfect Plan" instead of thoughts that are based in fear or assumptions and illusions that don't exist.

"Perfect Plan" moves us along even as we feel we're standing still. It speaks to the bigger picture, giving faith to all that has come before, all that will come after, and all that is in the present moment. "Perfect Plan" provides a knowing and a light, even at the darkest times. Through practicing "Perfect Plan" it becomes easy to recognize the enormous connection that's taking place throughout the universe.

We come with a birth date and death date and everything in between is our destiny. Embracing "Perfect Plan" does not give license to forgoing self effort. Do nothing and destiny will unfold as is. But employ self effort and the opportunity to change destiny is manifested.

Either way, we will come to an end ...and then we die. It's about how we get there. Build your foundation strong.

How to build a foundation with Perfect Plan? Repeat often.

Through good times... "Perfect Plan." Hard times... "Perfect Plan." Happy, sad... "Perfect Plan." Through all of life's trials and tribulations, successes, and celebrations. "Perfect Plan." Get the idea? After a while your mind will be trained to go there. To go to "Perfect Plan." "Perfect Plan" will replace fear as the bigger picture unfolds. After a while you will not need to practice. "Perfect Plan" will become habit. In crisis or chaos or just because, your mind will go there. Instead of a place of fear or angst, there will be calm as you move through life's ups and downs. Trusting in the "Perfect Plan" as the bigger picture unfolds. Acceptance in life's changes that all is as it should be, perfect, will be a given. The sometimes turbulent unknowing of why life is as it is, will soften with faith developed.

Trust it. Own it. Allow it to serve you. Build your faith and your foundation with "Perfect Plan."

Start The Conversation

The following pages are suggestions of questions and some answers to start the conversation on death and dying.

After each question, before reading on, take a minute to contemplate your responses.

- Which is more like death? Sunrise or sunset?
- Name a movie with a great death or dying scene.
- What would you choose for a last meal?
- Who would you like to meet you on your

journey when leaving your body?
- What music would you like played at your memorial service?
- What experience from this life would you like to go through eternity with?
- More to talk about...read on.

Sunrise or Sunset? A Riddle

*"For what is it to die
but to stand naked in the wind
and melt into the sun."*
-Kahlil Gibran

There is nothing in nature that has taught me more than the sunrise. It is a profound teacher in regard to death and dying.

So I ask, **"Which is more like death? A sunrise or a sunset?"** Both are glorious.

Most will say the sunset is more like death. Because when setting, the sun takes its rays of light with it, causing darkness. Which most liken to death. But this is more resembling of the soul contained in the body at birth.

It is the sunrise that is more like death. Upon rising, the sun's rays of light are set free, reaching everywhere. This resembles what happens when the soul leaves the body.

Practice Sunrise

A great practice to learn about what happens at death so you aren't frightened by the light that appears at your last breath, is to witness the sunrise. It could be at the ocean, in a field, on top of buildings, on a city street, perhaps on a mountain or desert, or even in a forest thick with trees. It doesn't matter where you are. There is a sunrise anywhere and everywhere in the world. Even when there are clouds or rain, the sun continues to rise. You can feel it even if you can't see it. Every single day.

Practice the sunrise by catching the first glimpse of morning light rising. To get the full benefit it is suggested to do alone. Stay very still. No talking, no walking, no taking pictures. Listen to the quiet of your own silence. Listen to only nature's voice. In this stillness at the moment of sunrise, briefly, effortless meditation takes place. All your cells align, and peace permeates throughout your body.

If you have identified a spot you can travel to easily every day, practice the sun rising there. In time, when closing your eyes, in any location at any given moment, you will be able to see that light within.

When it comes to dying, and you see the light, you will not only recognize it, but be drawn to it, comforted by the familiarity of the peace that was nurtured in the sunrise practice.

Movies

Name a Movie With a Great Death or Dying Scene.

The list of movies in this category is endless. The first ten movies sited below received the most repeat mentions from over one hundred people surveyed.

And the Oscar for best Death Movie goes to...

1. *Harold and Maude* 1971
2. *The Godfather* 1972
3. *Forrest Gump* 1994
4. *Saving Private Ryan* 1998
5. *Green Mile* 1999
6. *Hamilton* 2020
7. *Coco* 2017
8. *Dr. Zhivago* 1965
9. *Titanic* 1997
10. *Terms of Endearment* 1983

All the movies in this category are worth a watch and deserve honorable mention. They vary from heartfelt to horrifying. See how many you know and which are missing. All are good death and dying conversation starters.

Steel Magnolias * The Bridge * Defending Your Life * Departures * Death at a Funeral * Life is Beautiful * Up * Casablanca * Marley and Me * Bucket List * Lion King * Butch Cassidy and the Sundance Kid * Bambi * On Golden Pond * Philadelphia * Sunset Boulevard * Racing in the Rain * Gone With the Wind * Tombstone * Standing up Falling Down * Terminator 2: Judgment Day * Last of the Mohicans * Star Wars * The Land Before Time * Selma * Wrist Cutters * Rebel Without a Cause * My Sister's Keeper * One True Thing * Soul * Braveheart * On the Waterfront * Slum Dog Millionaire * Thelma and Louise * Twilight * King Kong * The Wizard of Oz * What's Eating Gilbert Grape * Shrek * Raiders of The Lost Arc * Hereafter * Harry Potter and the Deathly Hallows Part I and Part II * The Last Stop * Hatchico, a Dog's Tale * Psycho *

Moulin Rouge * Gran Torino * Brian's Song *
Bridge to Terabithia * Mrs. Miniver * Midnight
Cowboy * Avatar * Here Today * City of An-
gels * Sunshine Cleaning * The Elephant Man *
Full Metal Jacket * Beauty and the Beast * City
Slickers * Revolutionary Road * Far and Away
* Spider Man * Happy Gilmore * Finding Nemo
* Jaws * Brokeback Mountain * Legends of The
Fall * Bonnie and Clyde * Tim Burton's Corpse
Bride * Click * 7 pounds * Sixth Sense * My Girl
* West Side Story * Beaches * Scarface * Beautiful
Boy * Blade Runner * Point Break * Fearless *
The Hunger Games * Armageddon * The Dig *
Romeo and Juliet * The Shawshank Redemption *
A Walk to Remember * Mind The Gap * Old Yell-
er * Love Story * Meet Joe Black * Ghost * Grave
of the Fireflies * Jurassic Park * Princess Bride *
Alien * Dead Poets Society * Wolverine * Platoon
* The Lord of The Rings * Fatal Attraction * Little
Women * Pulp Fiction * Fried Green Tomatoes *
The Champ * The Notebook* American Beauty
* Boyz in The Hood * The Never Ending Story *
* Do The Right Thing *

A Change in Perspective

Science Fiction Disaster Movie to Romantic Love Story.

Lyle came to me in regard to the loss of his brother, which took place twenty-five years prior. At the time of his brother's death, he had an emotional shut down that he fed with all kinds of addictions. He came through, but still didn't know how to tackle the last bit. Lyle's inability to come to terms with sadness over his brother's painful death was still lingering making it hard to let him go.

When we began the work of evaluating Lyle's deep seated impressions surrounding death and dying, to the question of, "What is your favorite death movie?" Lyle responded, naming *Armageddon*, a science fiction, fantasy, end- of-the-world thriller. He explained, "When

Bruce Willis, in a moment of intense chaos and violence around him, sacrificed himself to save his son and the world." (That in itself, opens a can of worms as to who suffers more? The one sacrificing one's life, or the one left behind?)

After five months of death work, asked the same question, "What is your favorite death movie?" Lyle answered, *Ghost*. Also a fantasy thriller, but romantic in nature with a good dose of justice served. He explained why. "It was at the end, when Demi Moore, filled with love, let go, as Patrick Swayze went into the light." Once realizing that past unprocessed grief experiences were adding to the sadness of the loss of his brother, Lyle was also ready now, to let go.

Last Meals

What would you choose for a last meal?

The question began by asking about final life meal choices. Folks had so much trouble deciding, so the question shifted to, "If on death row, what would be the choice for a last meal?" Surrounding the question with an unlikely scenario seemed to make it easier for people to have answers. Food is a rich emotional trigger.

Personally I'm planning a smorgasbord.

(The numbers after the names reflect the age of respondent.)

- Breakfast! French toast, sausage, coffee, fruit, biscuits with jam. *Phil 83*
- Pozole. Tequila. *Lucy 53*
- Juicy steak, baked potato, pumpkin pie, Coke. *Claudia 39*

- Vodka gimlet on the rocks, fried calamari, eggplant parmesan, vanilla ice cream sundae. *Doreen 91*
- Chicken parmesan, pasta with garlic, garlic rolls, Tiramisu. *Antione 19*
- Cheeseburger, onion rings, warm apple pie with vanilla ice cream. *Lee 49*
- Flourless chocolate cake, chocolate mousse, death by chocolate ice cream with a scoop of chocolate mint. Top shelf tequila. *Bunny 67*
- Veal parmesan, angel hair pasta, bolognese sauce, garlic bread, Key Lime pie. *Ken 89*
- Sunnyside-up egg with melted cheese over sauteed vegetables, home fries, English muffin, cappuccino, blueberry danish. *Terry 27*
- Filet mignon with mushrooms and Bearnaise sauce, onion rings, sweet

potato fries, asparagus,   hot fudge sundae. *Elaine 87*

- Thanksgiving dinner. *Jesse 41*
- My mother's chicken fricassee with rice, fried green tomatoes, Blue Bell chocolate chip ice cream. Pepsi. *Jesus 52*
- Greek salad, dolmadakia, tzatziki with soft warm pita, spanakopita, boreks. *Yaya 42*
- Pork chops, butter peas, milkshake. *John 52*
- Lobster, coffee ice cream. Ellen 86.
- "Meatloaf with mashed potatoes and gravy, okra, and peach cobbler, and a slice or two of the Mrs. Homemade cornbread, if it wasn't too much trouble." - *John Coffey, death row inmate in the movie Green Mile - 1999.*

A Last Meal Story

We stayed up talking all night. Light was beginning to show itself when my brother said he was hungry. It was the first time in four days he showed an interest in food. "I'd love an Egg McMuffin." he said. I hadn't left him alone in weeks, but McDonald's was just a city block away. It was a simple wish to grant. I tucked him in as he drifted into sleep, and I pulled on my sneakers. With no time to waste I ran down eighteen flights of stairs, knowing that would be faster than waiting for an elevator. Hitting the ground floor running, I took flight to the golden arches.

It was about half an hour before opening. I could see the workers inside and knocked on the locked glass doors. Someone with a little seniority greeted me. I was in a hurry and didn't give him a chance to speak. I blurted, "I live around the corner with my brother who's dying. He asked for an Egg McMuffin. There's no time. I can't wait until you open. He's alone and asleep for the moment. I have to get right back. Please, I'll pay whatever."

He nodded. "Hold on." In moments, he was back with a bag. It was steaming hot with two Egg McMuffins and some hash browns.

"What do I owe you?" I asked.

"This one's on McDonald's." He winked and smiled kindly as I thanked him and took off in a sprint.

Not more than twenty minutes from when I left, back at my brother's side, I found him comfortably fast asleep. When he woke briefly, later in the day, he was no longer interested in the food he had desired earlier.

With a smile and gratitude, I thoroughly enjoyed the McMuffin. Meant to be a requested last meal for a dying man, I could taste the added secret ingredient – love.

The Game

Who do you want to meet on your journey?

The game, "Who do you want to meet on your journey?" is a great conversation starter about death and dying for anyone at any time. It gets the dialogue going between loved ones that otherwise might find themselves walking on eggshells about a topic that's hard to talk about.

The thought that your deceased loved ones, religious figures or heroes will be meeting you on your journey takes a little scare out of what's ahead, and believe or not, just the possibility of a companion, offers a bit of comfort on transition. When you ask the question, be ready to participate.

(First 100 surveyed)

34 – mother	3 – boyfriends or girlfriends
29 – father	3 - pets
9 – wives	2 – old flames
7 – husbands	1 - Gandhi
6 – children	1 – John Lennon
5 – siblings	

Old Flame Still Lit

Lena and I met at the Market over the cut flowers she was purchasing for a friend's funeral service. Our conversations about death and dying took off from there, as did our friendship.

She fought cancer for a few years, but when the effects of chemo and radiation forced her into a wheel chair, incontinent and unable to stand, she'd had enough. She called to ask if I could help her family work their way through her dying.

She had surrendered. There would be no hanging on, only letting go. And her acceptance and attitude made her loving family, who arrived from as far away as Israel, now surrounding her death bed, comfortable, sharing memories and laughs.

As family members gathered for a daily going away party, there was a joy for a life well lived. "Plenty of time to grieve after," she reminded and repeated to those around her.

Once when we were alone, I asked Lena, now bedridden, who she wanted to meet on her journey. She lit up as she spoke of a man she had met and loved briefly between husband number one and husband number two. In a whisper, looking towards the beyond, she told me about someone so different than any other. He taught her how to tango and fly a plane. He was a man that made her feel more sensuous than she had ever known. With Peter she could believe in all dreams coming true. Together they loved life. She never felt more alive. But their destinies weren't aligned and in sadness they went separate ways. That was over forty years ago. She had heard he died recently.

Loved ones lovingly kept showing up. A doting husband fed her, daughters changed her soiled bottom and a sister, nieces and nephews, grandchildren and friends all took turns, holding her hand, laughing and loving. Until the pain got worse and the morphine's release had Lena drifting into worlds unknown. It had been almost three days since we saw her eyes open or a response of any kind. Not a movement other than an occasional twitch. Family and friends gathered in the living room in waiting, taking turns one at a time, checking to see if Lena was still with us.

Sitting alone by her bedside, following the rhythm of her breath, I got close to her ear and whispered. "Lena, you're doing great. You're almost there. Peter is waiting." And with that, eyes still closed, a smile as big and broad as that of a Cheshire cat, lit up her face like the sun! For fear of giving her secret away, I had to hold back from laughing out loud.

When Lena passed forty minutes later, I'd like to think it was into the arms of the man she loved and wanted to meet on her journey.

Lena 1929-2017

One Day to Relive in Eternity

What experience from this life would you like to take through eternity?

Just suppose there was one day, one hour, even one moment you were instructed to pick from your lifetime to take through eternity. What would your choice for eternity be?

Sailing in the Caribbean with my wife. The wind is perfect. I can let go of the ropes and let it take us. With no effort the boat is sailing itself. I can feel the sun on my face and the breeze through my hair. The water is crystal clear, an aqua blue, and the Dolphins are swimming alongside. *Benjamin 63*

I was 14. It was the first perfect spring day, not a cloud in the sky. We could wear short sleeves and shorts. It must have been a weekend because there was no school. A group of us went to the beach to fly kites. I remember this one boy with his big smile that would light up his face in a boyish way and his eyes as blue as the sky that day. Somehow we paired together. The ocean crashed in the background. The seagulls danced along the shore. I know there were others with us, but they seemed to disappear. We laughed touching innocently and ran after a kite we playfully named. I fell in love for the first time that day. We became high school sweethearts. *Rachael 66*

Holding my newborn granddaughter in my arms while she slept. Rocking her on the gazebo swing looking out at the lake. Sky blue. Breeze balmy. Birds chirping, deer feeding. That would be my day to take into eternity. *Sylvie 52*

It's a toss-up. My climb in the southern alps of New Zealand on Mount Cook or a day of holding my friend's six-week-old in my lap. *Liz 59*

A perfect fall day, crisp, but not cold. Sitting on bleachers with good friends. Looking down at a field still covered with the soon-to-be-gone grass. Surrounding the field was a tree-lined border. It was at the peak of the most intensely magical array of vibrant autumn color marking the presence of divinity in its glory. It was a perfect moment in my life. I was happy in my marriage. I was happy in my work. In my community. My boys, two years apart, were playing soccer on the same team. And as

I watched them passing the ball to one another running down the field, I briefly felt I was in heaven. *Dorothy 71*

The day I hit a home run out of the park to win the game. I was a hero. *Clarence 49*

A day I would love to relive over and over! My kids and their kids – all together at a zipline on a mountain in Gilford, New Hampshire. The ride was thrilling, the view spectacular, but the best part was the family being together laughing, screaming and enjoying each others company! *Susie 75*

The birth of my first born. With both wives. *Robin 63*

Memorial Songs

What music would you like played at your memorial service?

Perhaps there is a song that makes your heart soar? Talks to you? Tells your story? Sheds light on who you are? Gives a message you want to leave behind? This is a simple but revealing question. What follows are the names and performers or writers of songs from people surveyed. "Amazing Grace" by far the most popular, was written in 1772 by John Newton after a near-death experience. It has been recorded over 6,600 times since then.

- "I Hope You Dance" – Lee Ann Womack, 2000
- "I Will Remember You" – Sarah McLachlan, 1993
- "I'll Fly Away" – Albert E. Brumley, 1929

- "Ripple" – Grateful Dead, 1970
- "Seasons of Love" – Jonathan Larson, 1996
- "My Way" – Frank Sinatra, 1969
- "Born To Be Wild" – Steppenwolf, 1968
- "Mr. Tambourine Man" – Bob Dylan, 1965
- "People Get Ready" – Curtis Mayfield, 1964
- "Wind Beneath My Wings" – Bette Midler, 1988
- "My Sweet Lord" – George Harrison, 1970
- "Circle" – Harry Chapin, 1972
- "Somewhere Over The Rainbow" – Judy Garland, 1939
- "The Answer's at The End" – George Harrison, 1975
- "You Raise Me Up" – Josh Groban, 2003

- "Don't Worry Be Happy" – Bobby McFerrin, 2018
- "Find The Cost of Freedom" – Crosby, Stills, Nash & Young, 1971
- "Love Song" – Elton John, 1970
- "Fire and Rain" – James Taylor, 1970
- "Prop Me Up Beside The Jukebox" – Joe Diffie, 1993
- "Through The Years" – Kenny Rogers, 1981 "
- "Grace is Gone" – Dave Matthews, Tim Reynolds, 2010
- "Streets of Philadelphia" – Bruce Springsteen, 1994
- "Keep Me In Your Heart For Awhile" – Warren Zevon, 2003
- "Song of the Heart" – Brian Crain, 2003
- "Supermarket Flowers" – Ed Sheeran, 2017
- "These Days" – Jackson Browne, 1967

- "The Last Song" – Elton John, 1992
- "You'll Never Walk Alone" – Rodgers & Hammerstein, 1945
- "Stairway to Heaven," Led Zeppelin, 1971
- "Bartender" Dave Mathews Band, 2002

More to Ponder

In Greek mythology sleep was called the twin brother of death. When asked, "If given the choice of how to die" most people choose "In their sleep." In spite of that being a predominate choice of death it's believed only about 12.4 percent of deaths take place while sleeping.

Asleep Before Eternity

We go to sleep believing we'll wake
although tomorrow may not come.
What if, unexpected,
you're one of the lucky ones
to slip away without tubes or bedpans
without commotion or chaos
suffering or sadness
without the holding to life?
Perhaps, your time
to be taken or to let go
will be deep beyond twilight into darkness
or at dawn before the cock crows.
Long or short duration
before the full sun has risen
and the moon has faded away.
Between sunset and sunrise.
All while sleepyheads dream
having yet to see
what awaits them in the light of day.
I wonder if there is a moment

while visiting places in your dreams
that you are met with a nudge
from the brain with a final command.
"It's time," the brain says.
"Breathe your last breath,"
and awaken to eternity.

In loving memory of Ellen R.
Age 54, no warning, gone in her sleep
1958-2012.

How Do You Feel About Your Death?

Most people said, "Don't know." Many answered, "Not afraid of death, afraid of dying." Three people responded: "Curious."

Others said:

* A little frightened, but excited. * Hopeful. * Like a small child waiting on line to see Santa. * I like sleep – so it will be a good nap. *

Afraid of pain. * A fabulous adventure! * Ready.
* Happy. * Sad. * I don't plan on it. * Can't wait!
* I'm going to need drugs. * Done. * Hoping it
comes before I become a burden. * I eagerly
await peace.

How do you want to disperse of your remains?

(First 100 surveyed)

41 – cremation,

32 – burial,

24 – undecided,

2 - at sea,

1 - left on a mountaintop

What do you fear most about dying?

Of the people asked, the answers of pain and incontinence just about tied. More specifically though, in dread of having a stranger wiping our . . .

Dreaded Moment

Wretched becomes this body
once to count on.
We can stand the pain just a little more
than the incontinence.
Letting go of life's simplest control
we are reminded we have nothing.

More To Talk About

Is there a historical event or moment that is death related that you vividly remember?

Recall the death of a great icon, a hero or celebrity. Why do these deaths stand out?

If you had a terminal illness and there was little or no hope of cure would you want to know the truth?

Would you want to know when the last day of your life was?

Complete this sentence:
If I knew I was going to die, I would . . .

Then do it!

VIII
In The End

There is no death you know this
the little voice that speaks to you
from yourself deep within knows.
"I won't die," it says
"I will live forever."
That's why no one believes.
Not the terminally ill on their deathbed
nor the men on death row with their death dates
not even those that watch as life becomes death.
Not doctors or nurses or caretakers
nor wives or husbands
nor lovers or soulmates or friends or family.
Not small children not any children.
No one believes death will come
for it will not.

March 15, 2020, and the COVID virus hits the fan.

Our business at the Market shifts while all non-essential others shut their doors indefinitely. We close the juice bar. Mathew is fired for refusing to wear gloves. Ruth bails, in protection of her ninety-eight year-old father at home. The news is bad. People over sixty-five are the target. Quarantine begins. With resistance I go home. My son swings into action as we enter a standstill of trade. Deliveries are stopped in their tracks. Adjustments are made to stock in coolers. Vendors are notified. We begin to address items like gloves, sanitizer, bleach, masks, online ordering, curbside pickup. A trailer is purchased for home delivery. And that is just the first week.

It is not business as usual.

Globally there wasn't a soul on the planet

unaffected. We all have our stories of survival and loss.

Perfect Plan? It's hard to accept with the deep sadness and suffering that has taken place coast to coast, continent to continent. There was no hiding from the devastation as the far reaching was brought into our living rooms any time we had the stomach to endure, day or night. But I still believe.

For me, if not for COVID this book never would have been written. I'd still be selling tomatoes. And for that I'm grateful, even though as I'm writing it, I'm not sure who it's for. It's been extremely cathartic, ironically to be reflecting on death experiences at the time of a world pandemic. There are many connect-the-dots of what happened and what continues to happen. We all must tell our stories.

COVID has felt a little reminiscent of the days of AIDS. A pandemic also caught in the crossfire of politics, fear, and misinformation. COVID was more far reaching as it was secretly spread airborne, sometimes by unsuspecting carriers, adding another horrible dimension. Not only were we unable to be with one another, every person, friend or stranger was suspect of potentially sharing a death sentence.

Fast forward. It's been over a year since that first day when alarms seemed to be going off worldwide. My son was working six days a week, holding down the fort. On the front lines, considered an essential worker, he lived in fear of being a possible carrier of a deadly virus when going home to his wife and three kids. Disrobing in a garage and showering before greeting the family members he lived for, the worry persisted. It was heartbreaking that he would have to stop his toddler from jumping in his arms. Absurd as it seemed, that this would protect her. It was a hard way to live.

In spite of the juice bar shutting down and the weeks we had to close when several employees tested positive, the Market reinvented with product that was in demand, survived with the help of government loans and a community that supported us. Once the vaccine emerged, it seemed one by one, we cautiously began to let our guard down. Business was delightfully picking up.

It had been a long haul. In this time of COVID many of us re-evaluated how we wanted to live our lives. I wouldn't be going back to the Market. It was time to answer a calling. And my son, at a crossroads at his midlife, knowing how time slips away, threw caution to the wind. With his wife, they made a decision to sell their home, buy an RV, and spend the next year as a family exploring the United States.

It was time to let go of the world we created with love, that took care of us and so many others for twenty years. Time to hand the torch over to some other blessed recipient.

With gratitude and a bitter sweetness, the decision came to close our Farmers Market doors.

One Last Story:
Ruthie

Ruth started working at the Market two weeks after my husband of thirty-three years and I split and two weeks before Valentine's Day. The biggest flower holiday, where sales of roses would go from three thousand stems per week to thirty thousand in a day. Between my uncontrollable crying in grief for the ending of a marriage and the intensity of revving up for what was coming, it's a wonder she stayed.

Ruthie and I became friends. Together we learned the flowers. Standing outside, out back, away from the buzz of the store. Under porch cover in the fresh air, we worked through the environmental challenges of rain or shine, heat or chill. Together through the years we wielded our box cutters, sleeved, taping, cutting, and creating flower bouquets out of God's palette of colors and design. At a table that served as our workspace, standing across from one another, positions of employer and employee lost boundaries. There, two very different women with nothing in common other than the certainty of our faith, albeit very differently sourced, cried, laughed, argued, shared pain and joy, trial, tribulation, celebration, and story.

Ruthie would travel one day, she mused out loud. Having fallen in love with the roses we prepped, she was eager to get to the Rose Bowl Parade in L.A. Year after year, she put it off for one excuse or another. I talked a lot of the book about death I would publish one day. Also with excuses, why it wasn't getting written. We both worked on the premise there was no time. A silly perceived reality. We talked about death - a

lot. And when I was called to a bedside, she covered my work and offered support so I could be
present with the dying without concern for the
Market. After, we'd reconvene, and while mind-
lessly prepping we'd share in the details of yet
another passing.

Ruth's 92-year-old Dad came to live with
her. As the years wore on, his care became more
consuming, and her dream of travel moved further out of reach.

COVID determined next moves. Early on,
Ruthie retreated home to protect her Dad, now
99. We didn't speak much throughout most
of that first year. Our conversations picked up
again when Ruthie's dad started failing and I
was able to help her through his end of life. We
planned a walk following the death.

But when that time came, Ruthie wasn't
feeling great. She had neglected a cough she had
developed a few months prior, while taking

care of her Father.

Finally, on antibiotics, after ten days passed and still no change, she returned to urgent care for an x-ray. Unable to catch her breath, she was checked into a hospital. Diagnosis took excruciatingly long. She was now breathless, on oxygen, and unable to speak. COVID tests, an MRI and finally a biopsy two weeks later revealed she had an aggressive cancer that would send her home with hospice to die. Her father gone, her work was complete. It was Ruth's time.

She wasn't conscious when I got to her bedside the very next morning. What to say? I was confident after years of discussion between us that she was neither afraid nor unprepared to do this. As the day wore on, I watched as death was taking my friend. Silently I cheered her on, knowing my loss would be painful. Letting her go, witnessing her final breath, was what I could do best for my Ruthie now. "Not at all what I had in mind Ruth — when we spoke of working together in death."

*In the end, you never know when
it will be the last time you see someone.*

In retrospect, I wished we had spoken more that isolating COVID year. I'm going to miss her. Her laugh her humor and her friendship. She was a good person. If she knew her death date would be sooner than later, I wonder if effort would have been made to get to the Rose Bowl. I want to believe she'll see it. Perhaps not watching from the ground, but there nonetheless.

*We mourn a piece of ourselves in the loss
of someone that defined us.*

For me, a part of myself will be missed with Ruthie's passing. She alone bears witness to the scope of the work I did with the flowers. That which I loved the most at my Farmers Market. I alone hold that memory now.

There were signs after she died.

A friendship ring I wore, lost four days before Ruthie's passing, mysteriously reappeared
in a bizarre place four days after her death. A
watch with a reminder of time, the same. Then
there were the two perfect purple roses, the
color Ruthie and I thought best for death, care-
lessly left at the store in a bucket of water, not in
a cooler where they belonged. I found them on
a Sunday when the Market was closed and I was
there to do paperwork. And lastly, for the moment... Ruthie's choice for a memorial song, not
once, but on three different radio stations when
getting into my car. Judy Collins, Ray Charles
and Willie Nelson singing individual renditions
of "Amazing Grace."[8]

Ruth 1958- 2021

---

8. "Amazing Grace," Christian hymn, 1779. By Clergyman John
Newton.

FINAL OPENING

It's somewhat nostalgic writing this on the last day that the doors opened at the Farmers Market.

I never returned during working hours after that ominous day on March 15, 2020. The day my son turned to me and with great urgency said, "Mom you have to get out of here! Go home and write your book." I left without looking back.

COVID was a sudden death for me. No time for closure. No time for good-byes. Things sitting on my desk left undone. But it also was an opportunity to unload twenty three boxes of what felt like a million pieces of paper that I had scribbled thoughts on about death and dying for the last twenty-five years.

Now on this last day, pages away from completion, I reflect on the "Perfect Plan" and with great excitement wonder what's to come?

If there was one moment to reflect on to-day as we say good-bye, and close our doors, it would be the daily act of opening the store. In particular the opening of the garage door that faced east and led out to the garden. In a glorious burst the sun welcomed the new day in perfect position, rising as if cued. Plants, that adorned the entrance, glistened rich with the morning dew. In support of hopefulness, rays of light would fill the market and set the tone for a beginning filled with possibility. As the brilliance entered inside, light spilled over the vibrant array of colorful fruits and vegetables bringing them to life.

As the day took off, the sun's entrance was followed by an endless stream of smiling fac-es. Familiar and unfamiliar, they brought with them more light and love, into the place, my own personal paradise, I called home for twen-ty years. It was here, I sold tomatoes.

Fun Farmer's Market Secrets

Woolbright Road, the home of our Farmers Market, is named for the family of Thomas Edward Woolbright Sr. (1875 to 1953), an Illinois coal miner who brought his wife and three sons to Boynton Beach, Florida, in 1912 to grow pineapples.

- Tomatoes should be free of blemishes and firm with a tiny bit of give when picked. They should smell earthy at the stem. Pink and even, rock-hard green tomatoes will ripen when left out in room temperature. Never put tomatoes in the fridge unless cut. It kills the taste. (Best to eat a whole tomato in one sitting).

- Cantaloupes should be left out of the fridge just long enough for the ends to soften up and a sweet scent to be detected. Chill first and then cut. Cold brings out sweetness in all melons.

- The silvery-white shine on the surface of grapes, blueberries, and some plums, known as the "bloom," acts as a protection against insects and is a sign of freshness. The bloom will fade when the fruit is handled or has age on it.

- You can't expect every item at the farmers market to be ready to eat when you purchase. Not cost effective, it would prove to be a financial nightmare and a huge waste of food for what would have to be tossed daily. Fruit that can be ripened (including tomatoes and avocados) after being picked needs to be timed. That doesn't include all fruit. Apples, citrus, and grapes are ready to eat when picked.

- Boiled eggs peel easily if cracked from the bigger end where there is always a little pocket of air. In order to keep eggs fresh, they are packed with the small end down which protects from bacteria. A spoiled egg will float in water.
- There are hundreds of varieties of potatoes. All with subtle differences. For mashed use a low starch like Yukon Golds. For hash browns and French fries use a starchier, drier Russet. The best for roasting are fingerlings.
- Hydrangeas don't like to be in a vase with other flowers.
- Never buy cut flowers with yellowing leaves. Watch for slimy stems or falling petals. It shows age.
- Watermelons are usually ripe if you can hear a hollow sound when tapping on it. Yellow on the underbelly where

it's rested on the ground is a good indication it wasn't picked too soon.

- The best artisan bread is made without dough conditioners and preservatives and is likely to mold within days without refrigeration.
- Asparagus is expensive because it takes two to three years to grow the first crop and farmers have to cover their costs.
- Cucumbers are best dark green and not too long or fat.
- It's a sulfuric compound that causes tears when chopping onions. Parsley gets rid of onion breath.
- Cook fresh corn soon after picking or purchase as the sugar in the kernels turn to starch rapidly and cause the corn to get tough and lose its sweetness.
- Avoid eggplants that are soft, shriveled or spotted.

- Since 2005 orange production has dropped 75 percent due to a disease called citrus greening (having nothing to do with the sometimes green color on oranges that is the result of not enough cold climate). In spite of the great decline, oranges are still Florida's biggest agricultural crop followed by tomatoes and sugar cane.
- Buying roses, check the freshness by gently squeezing the heads. (Too hard and you will bruise them.) They should have a firmness, indicating freshness, but never be as hard as a golf ball indicating the probability that the rose won't open.
- Cold-pressed juices may last between three to five days and longer, but lose some nutritional value after day one.

Whereas juice that is made with a fast juicer produces far less nutrients and loses nutritional value within an hour.

- Zucchini should be firm and free of cuts and bruises.
- Cherries with the stem intact are usually fresher.
- Flowers should be cut on an angle ensuring that water won't be limited by a stem sitting flat on the bottom of the vase.
- Mangos are not usually judged for ripeness by their color, but by squeezing. Ripe mangoes have a little give. There are over 500 varieties. (Many grow in the neighborhoods surrounding the Market.)
- Jalapeno peppers with stretch marks indicate hotter peppers.
- The heavier the lemon or lime, chances are the more juice. Lemons and Limes should be fragrant.

- Pineapples should smell sweet at the stem and be heavy for their size.
- Basil with black spots should be avoided.
- Check the bottom of the container when buying berries. It shouldn't be moist or stained. Don't wash berries until you're ready to use them. This will cause them to breakdown much faster.
- Tomatoes considered by most as a vegetable, are technically a fruit. Ninety-three percent of American gardening households grow tomatoes. Florida is the biggest grower and seller of fresh market tomatoes in the USA.
- With over 15,000 varieties, tomatoes are the most popular vegetable in the world.

"Short Long Life"

May your life be long, but feel short.
May your dying be met fearlessly.
May your death be a good one!

When Grandma Angel said these words, I understood what she meant right away. "Short Long Life." In the hard times it all feels so long. And when life is good, too short.

Live each day fully. Do the things you are putting off for tomorrow. Jump out of a plane, get a tattoo. See far off places or places close you've forgotten about. When was the last time you saw a sunrise? Make that phone call to an old friend you haven't spoken too in a very long time and say, "I love you" to the ones you love, often. Take advantage of the days you have, grateful for good heath, as that can be gone in a moment's diagnosis. Without warning, life so precious, can be fleeting.

Keep an eye on what lies ahead. Be prepared. Whether death comes swiftly, or by taking her time, either way, once she arrives there's no going back. Then it's just you and your self on a journey for unknown places unfolding.

Contemplate. Ask the questions that you have kept hidden, knowing they are there wanting, waiting to be answered. There is no coincidence that you read these words. How did you get here? And how will you move forward? "Perfect Plan."

Acknowledgments

W hen I was a small girl I remember thinking, *I'm going to write a book*. It seemed so simple at the time. I held that thought for over fifty years.

If not for the encouragement and support of three strong, beautiful women who grace my life in sisterhood, friendship, and love, I'm not sure this book would exist at all. Hali Layton, Ann Citron and Suzanne Alfandari. Thank you for endless conversations. For review. For the guidance to turn three hundred pages of grueling copy that read like a memoir into something someone might actually read. Thank you to Hali's honesty on the first draft – "I can't read this." (And for giving me a heartfelt fabulous cover design, as well as a thumbs up on the final, much shorter version.) Thank you to Annie's ability to be an endless sounding board offering reflective questions, with clarity and wisdom, that gave me direction and idea. "What do you want people to get from reading this? "What if ... ?" "Ask yourself ... " And thank you to Suzanne's unbridled enthusiasm, often exceeding my own, as she tried to correct my awful grammar and with kindness, temper my writing frustration. "You write like Yoda speaks." (I'm pretty sure she's the only one that got through those three hundred pages from cover to cover. I'm sorry Sue and very grateful.) For all the late nights and early mornings and all conversations leading back to death and dying, these three women have been guiding lights and rocks throughout my life. Thank you with all my heart.

To those whose paths have crossed with mine and are part of this book. To the many that aren't part of this book, but are a part of my story. To Maya S. for teaching me living while dying. To my dear Aunt Elaine Roberts, for a lifetime of love, caring, and availability, packed with eternal optimism. To Howard Goldfinger for his sense of humor and support early on, when I first realized my passion for Thanatology. To Karen Christensen and John Hines for getting me started, long before this project took off. To Susie Pope, whose candor and ability gave me much appreciated suggestions before the last revision. To Anita Finley for a serendipitous meeting at a pivotal time and an introduction to TriMark Press. Thank you all.

To Trimark Press – not only are they good

at what they do, they are good people. Thank you for taking me on *in spite of* Barry Chesler being not too excited about the subject matter and *because of* Lorie Greenspan's ability to see that "people really need this information." In particular, Lorie's kindness and patience goes unsurpassed. She was exactly the person "Tomatoes" needed – that I needed – to get this done.

And lastly, a mention and acknowledgment to my mom. For all the years she would ask, "When will you write your book?" To my return of, "What's the hurry? Death's not going away."

Here it is, Ma. No, Death's not going away and now we know, neither does it wait for anyone.

He searched
for his accustomed fear of death
and could not find it.
Where was death? What death?
There was no fear
because there was no death.
Instead of death there was light.
"So that's it!" he exclaimed.
"What bliss!"

Leo Tolstoy, 1886
The Death of Ivan Ilyich